HISTORY'S GREATEST WARRIORS

VIKINGS

RAIDERS AND EXPLORERS

Herald McKinley

Cavendish Square

New York

Published in 2015 by Cavendish Square Publishing, LLC
243 5th Avenue, Suite 136, New York, NY 10016

First Edition

Website: cavendishsq.com

CPSIA Compliance Information: Batch #WW15CSQ

Library of Congress Cataloging-in-Publication Data

McKinley, Herald.
Vikings : raiders and explorers / Herald McKinley.
pages cm. — (History's greatest warriors)
Includes bibliographical references and index.
ISBN 978-1-50260-117-9 (library binding) ISBN 978-1-50260-119-3 (ebook)
1. Vikings—Juvenile literature. I. Title.

DL66.M378 2015
948'.022—dc23

2014025538

Editor: Amy Hayes
Copy Editor: Cynthia Roby
Art Director: Jeffrey Talbot
Designer: Joseph Macri
Photo Researcher: J8 Media
Senior Production Manager: Jennifer Ryder-Talbot
Production Editor: David McNamara

The photographs in this book are used by permission and through the courtesy of: Cover photo by VisitBritain/John Coutts/Britain On View/Getty Images; William Brassey Hole/File:Battle_of_Largs_(Viking_ships_detail),_1263.JPG/ Wikimedia Commons, 4; en:User:Geogre/File:Peterborough.Chronicle.firstpage.jpg/Wikimedia Commons, 6; Print Collector/Hulton Archive/Getty Images, 8; W.G. Collingwood/File:Odin rides to Hel.jpg/Wikimedia Commons, 11; August Malmström/Wilhelm Meyer/Ristesson Ent./File:Vallhalla.jpg/Wikimedia Commons, 13; Baker, Emilie Kip/File:Valkyrie bearing Hero to Valhalla.jpg/Wikimedia Commons, 15; Leemage/Universal Images Group/Getty Images, 16; Viking/ The Bridgeman Art Library/Getty Images, 20; NTNU Vitenskapsmuseet/File:Hjelm_av_jern_fra_vikingtid_fra_Gjermundbu.jpg/Wikimedia Commons, 21; Wolfgang Sauber/File:Schonen-Wikinger Museum Foteviken 14.jpg/Wikimedia Commons, 21; Marieke Kuijjer/File:Runestone.jpg/Wikimedia Commons, 23; Skvattram/File:Runestone_Og211.jpg/ Wikimedia Commons, 25; Statens Arkiver – Danish State Archives/File:Jernalder (9288935543).jpg/Wikimedia Commons, 26; Christian Tønsberg/Peter Nicolai Arbo/File:Arbo-Olav_den_helliges_fall_i_slaget_på_Stiklestad.jpg/Wikimedia Commons, 28; Werner Forman/Universal Images Group/Getty Images. 30; Stephen Reid/Bridgeman Art Library/ Getty Images, 32; Nasjonalgalleriet Oslo/Christian Krohg/File:Christian-krohg-leiv-eriksson.jpg/Getty Images, 34; Print Collector/Hulton Archive/Getty Images, 36; Bridgeman Art Library/Getty Images, 38; Dagjoh/File:Burserydfunt1.jpg/ Wikimedia Commons, 40; Lgarciar/File:Wikingship.JPG/Wikimedia Commons, 41; Hofi0006/File:Wikingerschiff Oslo. jpg/Wikimedia Commons, 42.

Printed in the United States of America

CONTENTS

Vikings were fierce warriors known for their brutality.

The cold wind of the sea whips the long hair of the Norsemen. One of them spies something through the fog. Land! They have sailed from the Hardanger Fjord of Norway all the way to England. The warriors see a small village and dock their boats quietly. They grab their rounded shields and weapons. Each has an axe, a knife, or a spear. They are ready to fight.

A man comes out to greet them, unaware of how dangerous these travelers are. He stops to talk, and tells them about the ruler of the area. He tries to convince the Vikings to go to the king's house for trade. The Vikings, however, do not understand. They think he is insulting them, and now are ready to fight. They cut the man down, killing him in cold blood.

Even though they have just arrived, Viking warriors are making a fearsome example to the people of England. They are merciless, bloodthirsty, and ready to kill. As news of their exploits spreads, people begin to live in fear. Who could defend themselves against these half-crazed warriors, who hope that each battle will lead them to a gruesome end? The Vikings, fearsome warriors and skilled seamen, terrorize Northern Europe, pillaging any village too close to their longboats' reach.

Brittene igland is ehta hund mila lang.
7 twa hund brad. 7 her synd on þis
iglande fif geþeode. englisc. 7 brit
tisc. 7 wilsc. 7 scyttisc. 7 pyhtisc. 7
boc leden. Erest weron bugend þises
landes brittes. þa coman of armenia. 7 ge setan
suðewearde bryttene ærost. Þa gelamp hit þ pyh
tas coman suþan of scithian. mid langū scipū
na manegum. 7 þa coman ærost on norþ ybernian
up. 7 þær bædo scottas þ hi ðer mosten wunian. ac
hi noldan heom lyfan. forðan hi cwedon þa scottas.
we eow magon þeah hwaðere ræd gelæron. We witan
oþer egland her be eastan. þer ge magon eardian gif
ge willað. 7 gif hwa eow wið stent. we eow fultumiað. þ
ge hit magon ge gangan. Ða ferdon þa pihtas. 7 ge
ferdon þis land norþan weard. 7 suþan weard hit hef
don bryttas. swa we ær cwedon. And þa pyhtas heom abæ
don wif æt scottum. on þa ge rad þ hi ge curon heora
kyne cyn aa on þa wif healfa. þ hi heoldon swa lange
syððan. 7 þa ge lamp hit ymbe geara ryna. þ scotta
sum dæl ge wat of ybernian on bryttene. 7 þæs lan
des sum dæl ge eodon. 7 wes heora heretoga reoda ge
haten. fram þa heo synd ge nemnode dæl reodi. Six
tigum wintrum ær þe crist were acenned. gai iuli9
romana kasere mid hund ehtatigu scipū ge sohte
bryttene. þer he wes ærost ge swenced mid summum

KILLERS ON THE NORTHERN TIDES

Vikings were one of the most feared groups to have ever pillaged Europe. From the ninth to eleventh centuries, their brutality and great strength made them masters of a wide domain. The Vikings left behind very few written records of their deeds and culture, however. Despite their many gruesome accomplishments, **artifacts** of their culture are rare and unreliable. However, the image of strong, wild men with battle-axes is still remembered today. What do we really know about these ancient warriors?

For centuries, historians relied on a document called the *Anglo-Saxon*

Chronicle to teach us about the history of the Vikings. The *Chronicle* was compiled by English king Alfred the Great in 890 AD. It contains information about the Vikings' activities in Europe and their encounters with people living there. For instance, the *Chronicle* reported that in 789 an Englishman warmly greeted the newcomers who had arrived near his coastal home. The newcomers were Vikings. They killed the man immediately.

The attack on Lindisfarne, in 793, was considered especially vicious because the Vikings pillaged a monastery.

Without Regard for Sanctuary

In the eighth century, churches and **monasteries** were considered safe from attack. The monks, priests, and nuns who lived in them carried no weapons. They had no way of defending themselves against attackers. Because of this, they were a **sanctuary** from violence. Armies refused to attack churches because they believed these were holy places. Vikings, however, had no loyalty to the Christian church. They simply knew that churches and monasteries held gold and silver. The Vikings **raided** these places for all the treasure they could find.

Vikings also took people as their slaves. They often captured women and children, forcing them to work against their will. Some rowed the Vikings' boats. Others helped the Vikings set up new villages. Some slaves were allowed to farm. If these farms produced healthy crops, the slaves could buy their freedom.

More than Savage Warriors

The *Anglo-Saxon Chronicle* describes the Vikings mostly as savage warriors. In recent years, however, historians have discovered that Vikings did more than just raid and fight. As skilled traders, farmers, fishermen, and craftsmen, they made many of their tools from iron found in the bogs of Northern Europe. They were able to shape this iron into **sickles**, picks, and other tools.

Vikings have also been recognized as talented explorers. Sailing in their giant boats, they were able to reach regions as far away as North Africa. They traded their goods with Arab merchants, bringing back glass and spices. In other places, Vikings exchanged fur and slaves for precious metals. They worked these metals into beautiful rings, bracelets, and necklaces.

Odin rides upon his eight-legged horse, Sleipnir.

An Impressive Mythology

The Viking religion was based on the idea that there were many gods. These gods played an important role in Viking life. Vikings often asked these gods to help them through their difficult times and during their travels. Many stories were told about these powerful gods.

Odin, the god of war, wisdom, justice, and poetry, was the most powerful god in the Viking religion. He is often portrayed as having only one eye. Viking legends tell us that Odin gave up his other eye in exchange for wisdom. He also rode a horse that had eight legs and would never get tired.

Odin's eldest son, Thor the Thunderer, protected the universe. Thor was the god of sailors, farmers, and the sky. Able to control storms, Thor could even send powerful thunderbolts crashing to earth. Thor was famous for his hammer, *Mjollnir*, which means "the destroyer" in the Old Norse language. After Thor threw this weapon at an enemy, it would always magically return to his hand.

Many Vikings wore a silver hammer around their necks to honor Thor. He continues to be honored today in our calendars. This god's name is the basis of the word Thursday (Thor's day).

The End is Near

Viking **sagas** tell tales of fierce battles between the gods and enormous ice giants. Vikings believed the world would end with a fierce battle between the gods and these giants. This battle was called Ragnarök.

During the battle, it was believed that fire would break out and the world would be torn apart. According to the myth, a great wolf would swallow the sun. Only two humans would survive the terrible event. They would have to start a new world.

Valhalla was considered the Viking heaven, and only those who died in battle were admitted to its halls.

The Valkyries

Odin had nine daughters called the Valkyries. They flew over battlefields on winged horses and decided which Vikings would live or die.

Valkyries came to battlefields and gathered the souls of the bravest warriors who died in battle. These warriors, considered lucky and blessed, would be carried to Odin's banquet hall, Valhalla. There, the warriors would spend eternity feasting in Valhalla and fighting by Odin's side. It was said that only by dying on the battlefield could a warrior reach the heavenly halls of Valhalla.

The Valkyries carried the souls of the fallen warriors up to Valhalla.

Vikings were some of the best shipbuilders and sailors in the world. Some of them even crossed oceans!

Sailing the Seas

An essential part of the Viking culture was sailing. The Vikings were skilled sailors and boat builders. Their beautiful woodworking created impressive vessels, which they used both for exploring new land and for raids. The Viking boats were called **longships**, because of their long and narrow shape. Longships were very light and fast and could hold a crew of up to one hundred men. They were amazing feats of engineering.

Longships were made of long planks of overlapping timber. The timber was raised high in both the **prow** and **stern**, or front and back, of the boats. This style of building made Viking voyages over rough waters go more smoothly. Crossbeams were put in place for a deck and rowing benches. The Vikings put pine tar on the wood to make their longships waterproof.

The *drakar* was a type of longship used by Vikings to sail across the ocean. Drakars often featured a dragon's head carved into their prows. This fearsome decoration was a signal to their victims that they had come to fight. On their way to a raid, Vikings raised a square sail. This sail would catch high winds, pushing the Vikings across the sea. Once they got near their target, they lowered the sail and rowed the drakar with oars. Oars allowed Vikings to row through narrow passageways along a coastline. Drakars could be rowed right up to the beach. Once they landed, the crews could immediately launch their attacks.

Over time, Vikings developed other types of ships. One of these was the *knarr*.

The knarr was higher and wider than a longship and had fewer oars. It was able to hold massive amounts of cargo. Vikings used this ship when trading over great distances.

Weapons Worthy of Vikings

Vikings were always prepared for battle. They used axes, spears, and swords during combat. A sword's handle was often decorated with precious metals. Viking warriors preferred using double-edged swords. This way, they knew they would wound their enemies no matter which side of the sword struck them.

The battle-axe may be the most well known Viking weapon. Two types of battle-axes were used by these warriors.

These axes on exhibit at the Museum of London were made from wood and iron.

One was held in the hand and swung at enemies. A lighter axe was thrown with tremendous force. Blows from battle-axes were usually fatal. Vikings were also known for using spears and knives. The most skilled warriors could throw two spears at once. Some Vikings could even catch an enemy's spear in flight and hurl it back.

The Wardrobe of a Warrior

Vikings almost always engaged in hand-to-hand combat. During this type of fighting, Vikings used circular shields to protect themselves. Their shields were made of wood and leather and had iron handgrips. They were often painted in bright colors. Around the year 1000, these shields were redesigned. Vikings began building their shields in the shape of kites, which gave better protection to the warriors' legs. Vikings used helmets made of leather or metal to protect their heads from injury. Metal helmets featured nose guards for extra protection. However, these helmets were not topped with horns, as many people believe.

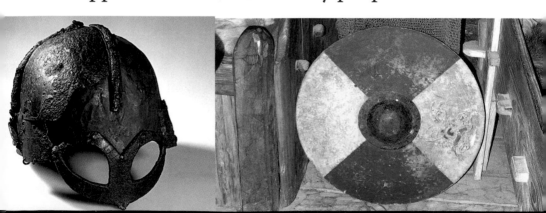

An early Viking may have carried a shield similar to this, while a later Viking wore a helmet like the one above.

A Violent Education

Viking boys often followed in their fathers' footsteps. If their fathers had been trained as warriors, they would receive the same training. They grew up learning the skills required for waging war. They spent more time wrestling than learning arithmetic. Viking elders shared many myths about war heroes who conquered land and claimed treasure. Young warriors hoped that by serving important leaders, they would be rewarded with their own fame and wealth.

Governments and Arguments

Vikings usually did not have a formal government or written laws. Instead, they held local meetings where they discussed common interests. At some of these meetings, Vikings would share information about hunting and fishing with one another. More often, these meetings were held to settle fights or disputes between Vikings. This was usually done with money. If money didn't solve the problem, the Viking being **punished** would be **banished**. As a last resort, the arguing parties would duel to the death.

Mystical Letters

The Vikings did not use the same alphabet we use today. They used a form of lettering called **runes**. With no paper to write on, Vikings **chiseled** runes into stone and other objects. They deeply respected runes, believing them to be a gift from Odin. It was believed that anyone who could read runes had the power to cure illnesses and break through chains.

Runes often were placed in complicated designs, emphasizing the importance of the words.

Runes did not always stand for specific letters, and were used for many reasons. Vikings labeled their personal belongings with them. It was believed that carving runes into weapons made them more powerful.

After a successful raid, Vikings often carved runes into statues in the town. Runes were also carved into memorial stones to honor warriors killed in battle. Now considered an important source of Viking history, almost three thousand of these stones have been found in Scandinavia.

This runestone is located north of Mantorp, in Sweden.

Jernalder

A Viking ship with shields displayed was a frightening sight.

CHAPTER THREE

FIGHTERS AND EXPLORERS

On a Boat

Vikings started their raids in early summer. Sailing to a raid, Viking crews hung dozens of shields on the sides of their longships. The shields helped protect the crews from enemy arrows, but they also had another, more sinister purpose. The shields signaled that the Vikings were coming to attack, and were used to scare the crews' enemies as the longships sailed to shore. Displaying these threatening and purposeful shields was an important way to get warriors excited to fight.

Although Vikings rarely battled on the open seas, they were always prepared to do so. If Viking warriors spotted enemy ships closing in, they'd bind their fleet of longships together with thick rope. Once the enemy drew close enough, the Viking fleet would launch a shower of arrows and spears at their ships.

The best Viking warriors stood at the ship's prow. As the enemy drew closer, these warriors leaped onto their ships. The Vikings weren't trying to sink the enemy vessels. They were trying to capture them. They were also looking for any treasures stored on board.

Viking battles were disorganized but often their element of surprise won them victory on the battlefield.

Viking Battle Moves

Most Viking battles, however, took place on land. Once their longships reached shore, the Vikings went after their surprised victims. Their style of fighting was very disorganized, however, so Vikings preferred sneak attacks. When they fought large battles against well-trained armies, they usually weren't as successful.

Still, the Vikings did use a few fighting strategies. Once they reached the shore, the youngest Vikings often formed a **front line**. Each overlapped his shield with the shield of the warrior standing beside him. In this way, they formed a solid wall that protected the more experienced Vikings from enemy arrows. One Viking would throw a spear over enemy lines to dedicate the battle to Odin. Then, they showered sharp spears on the enemy.

Vikings also used a formation called the *svinfylking*. Vikings used this formation to overpower their enemies. About thirty Vikings would line up in the shape of a

"V" with the point of the "V" facing the enemy. All at once, the Vikings would charge, trying to break through enemy lines with their great weight and numbers.

Viking warriors known as berserkers channeled animals to make them fiercer in a fight.

Berserk Berserkers

No Vikings fought as wildly as the Berserkers, who painted their faces before fights. Some reports say they dressed like wild animals, wearing hides instead of clothes or armor, while some claim the

Berserkers fought naked. All the legends agree that Berserkers acted like wild animals. They would work themselves into a state of rage before a raid began. They'd start to shiver, and their teeth would chatter. While in this vicious state, they bit off pieces of their own shields and howled like wolves. During battle, Berserkers were able to ignore pain.

This fierceness shocked their victims, and often was so scary that people surrendered without a fight. Although the Berserkers were considered some of the best fighters, other Vikings did not like them. Berserkers would be so blind during their battle rage that they would attack their **allies**. In 1015, a group of Vikings outlawed Berserkers.

A Red-Bearded Man in Greenland

Erik the Red was considered one of the greatest Viking leaders and explorers. As a young boy, Erik's father killed a man during an argument in Norway. Erik and his family were cast out of their homeland, and were forced to move to Iceland.

After a few years of living in Iceland, Erik the Red got into a heated fight. It is believed he killed two men during the fight. A Viking elder found him guilty of the crime and, like his father, Erik was banished from his home. Rounding up a group of friends, Erik then sailed west of Iceland. His crew soon discovered new land on the tip of Greenland. Most of it

Erik the Red (right), one of the most famous Vikings, is known for discovering Greenland.

was covered with **glaciers**. The dirt was frozen. However, Erik found land near the sea that he was able to farm.

Erik the Red's punishment ended three years later. He returned to Iceland, hoping to convince people to join him in the new land he had discovered. He called this place Greenland, believing this name would convince others to join him. Erik's trick worked. Many Vikings followed Erik to Greenland. Thanks to Erik the Red's leadership, Greenland's population soared for many years.

The Lucky Leif

Born around 980, Leif Eriksson was Erik the Red's son. Like many Viking boys, Leif spent much of his childhood apart from his family. From an early age, boys were trained to become strong, fierce warriors.

At the age of eight, Leif began studying with a man named Thyrker. Thyrker was a German whom Erik the Red had captured during a raid. Thyrker taught Leif how

Christian Krohg's depiction of Leif Eriksson (right) discovering North America.

to read and write, to trade goods, and to speak in different languages. Most of all, he taught Leif to become a fearless warrior.

After his training, Leif set sail on many voyages. During a trip home to Greenland, he saved a crew whose ship had been in a wreck. Leif was given the ship's cargo as a reward. For this, he became known as Leif the Lucky.

Leif's most famous journey took him to the North American continent. He was the first European to land there, nearly five hundred years before Christopher Columbus. Experts have different opinions about why Leif made this trip. Some claim that his ship was simply blown off course. Others suggest that Leif heard about North America from a fellow Viking sailor.

Whatever the case, Leif probably reached North America around the year 1000. He found a coast filled with meadows, trees, and wild grapes. Leif's luck had struck again! He named this new land Vinland. Historians believe that Leif's crew landed on the northern tip of what is now called Newfoundland, an island off the coast of Canada.

RAIDER'S TIP

Some villagers were so afraid of raids that their leaders paid off the Vikings in advance.

Vikings decided to convert to Christianity. This painting depicts the Baptism of Rollo at Rouen.

Christian Conversion

Vikings came in contact with a variety of different peoples during their explorations. Many times the Vikings attacked these peoples, but sometimes they also met and traded with them. Vikings received more than goods and gold in these meetings. They learned and **co-opted** the ideas and beliefs of these new cultures as they saw fit.

In 984, Leif Eriksson sailed to Norway. He brought gifts to Norway's ruler, King Olaf. Olaf told Leif that a terrible disease had swept across his land.

Many of his people died from the disease. Once the king **converted** to the Christian faith, the disease ended. Moved by this change in fortune, Leif decided to start following this new faith as well.

The Vikings were happy to accept the Christian faith. For them, this decision simply meant believing in one more god. It also helped the Vikings make more money, since Christians would not trade with those who didn't share their faith. Once Vikings accepted this new religion, Christians began to trade freely with them.

The Battle of Stamford Bridge, which took place in 1066, ended with the Vikings fleeing England.

The Battle for England

The Vikings had been battling for control of England for many years. In the ninth century, the Vikings were forced away from western England. However, they took England back in 1016, led by their king, Knut. Their control of the country only lasted a short time, however, and they were driven out in 1042.

In 1066, Vikings tried reconquering England. They raided coastal villages in the north and captured the town of York. England's King Harold sent most of his army to stop the invaders. A fierce battle was fought in York as the English army destroyed the Viking forces. The Vikings never mounted another significant raid against England. The end of the Viking era was near.

A change in the style of combat also led to the end of the Viking era. It became common for towns to pay soldiers for protection. Villages that were once defenseless now had armies at their command. These trained soldiers were much more prepared for Viking sneak attacks. They rode on horseback and were heavily armed. Viking warriors found they had met their match.

This baptismal font is a perfect example of how Viking culture incorporated Christianity.

Historians learn a lot about Viking culture by studying the carvings on the remains of Viking ships like this one.

Clues to the Past

Vikings didn't record things on paper. Instead, they carved runes into stones. Vikings left behind few written records because of this, and most of the stones that have been found give only brief accounts of historical events. To learn about Viking culture, we have to examine other artifacts the Vikings left behind.

Archaeologists have uncovered many items used by Vikings, including beautiful pieces of jewelry, weapons, fabric, and even entire Viking longships! Two ships, the *Gokstad* and the *Tune*, were found in very good condition and have taught us a lot about Viking culture. The ships were unearthed in Norway in 1880 and 1906.

This nearly intact Viking longship is on display in a museum in Oslo.

The ships had been purposely buried in pits of waterlogged clay and covered with stones and earth. Archaeologists believe that the bodies of dead Vikings were put on the ships, which were then buried. We do not know who the dead were, but perhaps they belonged to a royal family. Animal remains, cooking tools, beds, and tents were also found on the ships. Archaeologists hope to determine if burying the dead in this way was a common practice in Viking culture.

Many people go and visit these ships at the Viking Ship Museum in Oslo, Norway. People are learning new information about the Viking warriors every day. Through continued study, perhaps we may be able to know more about these fierce warriors and their exciting world.

GLOSSARY

ally A person or organization that cooperates with or helps another.

archaeologist A person who learns about the past by digging up old objects and examining them carefully.

artifact An object used by people in the past that gives archaeologists clues to their culture and environment.

banish To send someone away from a place and order the person not to return.

chisel To chip away at something and form it into a desired shape.

chronicle A detailed recording of historical events.

conversion The process of changing from one religion to another.

co-opt To take into a group.

front line The line or zone of contact with an enemy.

glacier A huge sheet of ice found in mountain valleys or polar regions.

longship A long, narrow ship with many oars and a sail, used especially by the Vikings.

monastery A group of buildings in which monks live and work.

prow The bow or front part of a boat or ship.

raid A sudden, surprise attack on a place.

rune A letter in the written alphabet of the Vikings, usually carved onto stones.

saga A long story about heroes and events passed down through generations.

sanctuary A holy place that offers safety or protection.

sickle A tool with a short handle and curved blade that is used for cutting grain, grass, or weeds.

stern The back end of a boat or ship.

FIND OUT MORE

Books

Jovinelly, Joann, and Jason Netelkos. *The Crafts and Culture of the Vikings.* New York, NY: Rosen Publishing Group, Inc., 2003.

Lassieur, Allison. *The Vikings.* Farmington Hills, MI: Lucent Books, 2001.

Margeson, Susan M. *Viking.* DK Eyewitness Books. London, UK: DK Publishing, Inc., 2010.

Steele, Philip. *Hands-On History: Viking World.* Leicester, UK: Armadillo Books, Inc., 2013.

Websites

Hurstwic: Viking History
www.hurstwic.org/history/text/history.htm#Society
Learn more about the Viking age through links to factual articles regularly updated and stored on this website.

PBS: NOVA Online
www.pbs.org/wgbh/nova/ancient/volga-trade.html
Discover why many experts believe that the Volga trade route supplied Vikings with prized crucible steel, and find out the secrets of Viking ships.

Smithsonian National Museum of Natural History: Vikings: The North Atlantic Saga
www.mnh.si.edu/vikings/start.html
Sail the stormy seas in your own longship through this interactive website, and retrace the voyages of discovery and settlement to find the answers.

INDEX

Page numbers in **boldface** are illustrations.